The Plague of Love

Praise for

THE PLAGUE OF LOVE

Like Mir, Shaw and Lee have taken a classic text and recast it in the furnace of their imaginations. Here is a Mir never seen in English before, witty, rhetorically complex, embodying passion, and making us laugh painfully with his skillfully deployed humor. Here are his poems, no longer receding into the past like ships in the mist, no longer separated from us by the veil of language. They sprout from the ground with color and energy, and in this book, reinvented, they live.

--Tony Barnstone,, Professor of English Whittier College, Poet, Author, co-translator of *Faces Hidden in the Dust: Selected Ghazals of Ghalib*

Rendered hemistich by hemistich, Mir's verses come alive with the poet's aesthetic vitalities, his two worlds – the mundane and the divine, his philosophy of love and life. The translations carry a certain aura of light and shade emanating from the original Mir text. The joy these translations offer lies not so much in transcending the strict bonds of the ghazal artifice as in the enhancement of the virtues of what is being said. Their excellence emerges from free versions, escape from self-indulgence; commendable.

The translators have attempted the primacy of the original and sustained fidelity with passion and precision.

-- Bhupender Parihar Aziz, Urdu poet and translator, author, *Ghalib: Decolonizing Meaning*

Nirala Series

THE PLAGUE OF LOVE

Bilal A. Shaw is a Kashmiri-American scientist who completed his Ph.D. from the University of Southern California in quantum information science. He studied Mathematics at Whittier College, California. In the past he has worked on DNA-based computation, software architecture, and theoretical self-assembly. Currently he works as a senior director of data-science in identity and fraud analytics at Transunion. With Tony Barnstone he recently published *Faces Hidden in the Dust: Selected Ghazals of Ghalib* (White Pine Press, 2022). Some of these ghazals have been published in *Literary Matters, Able Muse, Arroyo Literary Review,* and *Pratik.* He currently lives and works in Santa Monica, California.

Anthony A. Lee, Ph.D. (History, UCLA, 2007) is retired as a lecturer in African American history at UCLA and now continues his research as an independent scholar. He is the General Editor of the academic series, Studies in the Babi and Baha'i Religions (Kalimat Press, 1982-), now in its twenty-eighth volume. He translated, with Amin Banani and Jascha Kessler, *Tahirih: A Portrait in Poetry: Selected Poems of Qurratu'l-'Ayn* (Kalimat Press, 2005). Also with Amin Banani, *Rumi: 53 Secrets from the Tavern of Love* (White Cloud Press, 2014); with Nesreen *Akhtarkhavari, Love Is My Savior: Arabic Poems of Rumi* (MSU Press, 2016), *Wine of Reunion: Arabic Poems of Rumi* (MSU Press, 2017), and *Desert Sorrows: Poems of Tayseer al-Sboul* (MSU Press: 2015).

THE PLAGUE OF LOVE

Selected Sufi Love Poems of Mir Taqi Mir

MIR MUHAMMAD TAQI

Translated from Urdu by

Bilal A. Shaw & Anthony A. Lee

Nirala

Nirala Publications
Third Floor, 310, Hari Sadan,
Daryaganj, New Delhi-110002
niralabooks@yahoo.co.in
www.niralapublications.com

First Edition 2023

ISBN : 978-81-963601-0-8

Cover Design: Graphical House

Printed at
Chaman Offset New Delhi-2

Foreword

Tony Barnstone

This remarkable translation of the poems of Mir does the core work of re-creation, not just replication. Two poets, using all of their heart and imagination, embody in their versions not just the meaning of the poems, but also the action that the poem takes when engaged with the mind. If a poem is as William Carlos Williams wrote "a machine made out of words," that machine is constructed out of component parts, and those parts when activated and engaged with each other perform work. That work is not just the carrying of the load of meaning, as if the poem were a kind of verbal bucket. It's more like a wheelbarrow, constructed of three simple tools: the lever, the barrel, and the wheel. One of them lifts the load, the other one carries the load, and the third one transports the load. So, the translation of that poem had better lift, carry, and transport, or it will simply bring across the meaning without bringing across the function of the poem—It will translate all the poetry out of the poem, all in the name of fidelity.

In *The Plague of Love,* the translators do this essential work. These are poems in English, ones that embody the abstract and emotional in images so powerful that they are almost surreal. Here, for example, is the tortured lover, dead inside yet still pathetically offering bouquets in hopes of requital:

Now, flowers push up through my hollow eyes,
my hands hold daffodils in bright bouquets.[1]

Here is the lover carrying the wounds of love in his mind as if they were marks on his body: "These love stains on my skin will not come off" and "This love-burn scars my heart." Often this embodiment of emotion manifests itself through precisely observed and powerful metaphor and simile: "Like tinkling bells of caravans, / far from you, loneliness is mine." In these ways, Mir threads the needle between his use of traditional images of love and despair and the renewal of those images through placing them in bodies and things, to make them present to the mind and heart. As E.L. Doctorow writes, "Good writing is supposed to evoke sensation in the reader—not the fact that it is raining, but the feeling of being rained upon."

Often, that manifestation of abstractions in the body spills out of the self onto the landscape, as if the heart were a movie projector spraying emotions onto the screen of the world:

I'll leave this world in tears, wailing.
When I'm gone, for me clouds will weep.[2]

or,

I wrote a verse for you on every leaf.
And Spring itself was envious, I know.[3]

Our term in the West for this is the "pathetic fallacy," and it comes from the idea that the self is not a lamp but a mirror, that we can reflect the world, but we can't change it by projecting ourselves onto it. Yet in Mir, nature is intimately entangled with human nature, and the whole world feels with the poet: "If I cry, Earth and Air will burn. / The blue slope of the sky will burn." The poet is a spirit animating the landscape; similarly, the whole world seems to be inside the poet: "My eyes and heart now boil in agony. / Fire and water in one riverbed." In fact, the sense of despair that the poet feels from unrequited love is so intense that it is manifested in the poem as an apocalyptic, world-ending event: "Don't ask Mir of love's cruelty. / If he cries, the cosmos will burn."

Another tool that Mir uses is a remarkable irony and wit. Sometimes this manifests as an inverted parallelism:

> You knew a hundred just like me,
> but I could find no one like you.[4]

Other times he deploys it through a use of repetition and variation: "You are naïve if you think she's naïve," or through a kind of understated, despairing humor:

> Should I kill someone or slit my own throat?
> My tongue replies: Yes. You must do something.[5]

Like the great comic writers, Mir switches back and forth between such ironic understatement and a heightened hyperbole, a kind of bipolar rhetoric that avoids the calm center. The cruel lover shoots "A hundred arrows from her eyelashes," she flays some of her suitors, and tortures others "at the stake." The use of such comic methods keeps us off-center, vulnerable to the poem's intense emotion.

Another technique Mir uses is to recycle traditional images of love-pain such as that of Majnun, the heroic lover in Persian literature who wandered the desert in a kind of divine madness, pining away for his lost lover, *Layli*. So, Mir presents himself as a broken house and the world as a wasteland, asking,

> Mir, who can ever live in this wasteland?
> Walls, doors fallen. The houses in despair.[6]

It is a cliché, yet he deploys another cliché, that of the lover weeping tears of blood, to renew both tropes:

> If my tears of blood fall on this wasteland,
> this desert dust would bloom again with haste.[7]

So, he hybridizes the menagerie of oft-repeated images,

and creates something new under the sun, like a lion-badger or a rabbit-fox. It is a kind of irreverence with which he approaches all traditions, even religion:

Why ask Mir his creed? Praying in the temple,
caste mark on his brow, he's left Islam now.[8]

Though he presents himself as an "infidel," he does so to make a new religion: "The first one to make love his creed, he was," worshipping the lover as his new idol.

Like Mir, Shaw and Lee have taken a classic text and recast it in the furnace of their imaginations. Here is a Mir never seen in English before, witty, rhetorically complex, embodying passion, and making us laugh painfully with his skillfully deployed humor. Here are his poems, no longer receding into the past like ships in the mist, no longer separated from us by the veil of language. They sprout from the ground with color and energy, and in this book, reinvented, they live.

References

[1] "My Heart Dims," p. 100.

[2] "Wipe your Tears," p. 70.

[3] "Mir's Poems," p. 64.

[4] "I Waited," p. 52.

[5] "Do Something," p. 43.

[6] "Wasteland," p. 84.

[7] "Love and Faith." p. 86.

[8] "Finished," p. 97.

Translating Mir Taqi Mir

Bilal A. Shaw & Anthony A. Lee

What is poetry? The question is often asked but has never been adequately answered. It has vexed poets and scholars alike. That is the uncomfortable, the intolerable place where every translation of poetry must begin.

In every language, in every society, and in every culture, there is a body of poems that has withstood the test of time. These are often religious texts, or mystical works, that embody the deepest values of a culture. Yet in our own time, thousands – if not millions – of poems are written every day by ordinary people and by great authors. Almost immediately, they are forgotten. So, perhaps the real question is: What is *not* poetry? What is the difference between poetry and mere rhyming, or prose? Why does a true poem endure?

This volume is an attempt to bring a selection of the poems of Mir Taqi Mir (1723-1810), an important eighteenth-century

Urdu poet, into English. But how is such a thing possible? Every poem is a unique combination of words that cannot be altered, even in the original language, without destroying the work. How can a poem be transported across languages, across cultures, and across centuries of time and remain intact, preserving the beauty of the original? We must admit that very often these attempts fail. They result in a slack prose that does not resemble poetry at all.

Poetry is the language that we use when there is no language to convey the emotions, the insights, and the spiritual states that are beyond description, but that we as human beings experience. It is an attempt to capture in words experiences and feelings that are beyond words. Poetry moves beyond language. It cannot explain, it can only point the reader in the right direction.

As such, the bare words of the poem are not enough. The poem, if successful, must catapult the reader, or the listener, into the same emotional state that the poet has experienced. It is this element of a poem, the essential element, that can be translated across languages. It is this timeless, ephemeral aspect of each poem that the poet-translator must experience, understand, and convey in a new language and to a new and foreign audience. But this aspect of the poem is universal. It is the essence of poetry itself and so it can be conveyed. An ancient string of words can magically come to life, become meaningful, and even deeply personal. The right translation can teleport meaning between cultures, find common themes in languages, and share experiences across time and across space. It is here that translation can connect different peoples and nations and testify to the unity of humanity.

This volume is an attempt to render into English a selection of Mir Taqi Mir's Urdu poems and verses, in language that captures at least some of the power and excitement of the originals. Mir's Urdu poems have rarely been translated into

English, and almost never with much success.

The value of Mir Taqi Mir's eighteenth-century verse has survived the test of time. He is recognized as the most powerful writer of Urdu love poetry. The problem that confronts the translator is how to bring these Urdu verses into English in language that will retain that power. The selected Urdu poems in this book are highly compressed expressions of ideas about love written in the context of Sufi mystical teaching and Islamic culture. They refer to spiritual themes, employ cultural tropes, use erotic images, and make references to Quranic verses that are unfamiliar to most English readers.

The challenge for any translation of poetry is to bring a poem from one language and culture into another language and culture, while remaining true to both the spirit and the meaning of the original. In this effort, a word-for-word translation is no help at all, and this book makes no attempt at that. Moreover, a translation that provides only the meaning of a poem, while it may give a thorough understanding of what the poet said, translates nothing of the beauty or excitement of the original. It loses the poem altogether, replacing it with a dull explanation. The worst outcome of any translation of poetry would be to take a poem that sounds natural, urgent, and transcendent in its original language and render it into English prose or flaccid poetry that is dull, ponderous, and awkward.

The Life of Mir

Mir Taqi Mir was the first of the great poets of Urdu. He was also the most prolific. His works include more than 13,500 couplets, made up of more than 27,000 lines of poetry. His poems span many traditional genres, including *rubaiyat* (quatrains), *masnavi* (long rhymed narratives), *qasida* (lyric odes), and the *ghazal*. However, most of his poems are ghazals. He is regarded as the master of the Urdu ghazal. His distinctive style and language, blending Persian poetics with ordinary Urdu created a pattern of Urdu ghazal that has been imitated by subsequent generations of poets.[1] All great Urdu poets have paid homage to Mir in their work, including Urdu's greatest poet, Ghalib, who writes:

> You are not the only master of *rekhta*,[2] Ghalib.
> In days past, there used to be someone called Mir.

Born Mir Muhammad Taqi in Agra (then Akbarabad), he used simply "Mir" in all of his poems as a nom de plume. Mir's father was a Sufi mystic who spent his life in pursuit of spiritual truth and remembrance of God. He passed his mystic attitudes on to his son, impressing him with the teaching that love is the most powerful force in the universe. Such Sufi teachings are evident in all of Mir's poems. Mir's father died early in Mir's life, perhaps before he was a teenager. Though his father had a large following, he apparently left his son nothing. Mir's stepbrothers took control of their father's estate, and he was left in the care of his paternal and maternal step-uncles.

As he says in his poems, his life from then on was a string of tragedies. In two long poems (*masnavis*)[3], which are probably autobiographical, Mir relates two early love affairs. The first seems to have been a casual and happy relationship that was short lived. The second affair was catastrophic. He became involved with a young, married woman whom he loved to the point of obsession. When the affair was discovered, his family was outraged. He was denounced by his brothers and forced to travel to Delhi to find a protector. His grief carried him to the brink of madness. References to these sad events can be found in many of Mir's poems. His early experience of love seems to have left deep wounds, so that love and calamity are forever linked in his psyche. Mir goes on loving but love and pain are inseparable.

In Delhi, Mir was accepted by the ruler and given a stipend as a court poet. He became well known and widely celebrated. But he witnessed repeated attacks on the city that brought about the slaughter of many residents, much destruction, and widespread looting. The city became a ruin of its former greatness. He was given refuge in the home of his stepbrother's maternal uncle. This arrangement came to an end when his stepbrother informed his uncle of Mir's adulterous affair in Agra and advised him to show him no courtesy and give him no assistance. Unable to return to his native city, Mir eventually made his way to Lucknow.

By the time Mir arrived in Lucknow in 1782, his fame as a poet was well established. The rulers of the city offered him a generous allowance to remain in the court as a poet. However, in Lucknow its rulers regarded poetry as a sort of light entertainment rather than a high art. Mir did not receive the respect he expected as a serious poet with something to say. He constantly took umbrage at his treatment at court. Mir insisted on maintaining his dignity and demanded respect from a succession of patrons with whom he had stormy relationships. When he died in 1810, he had separated himself from the court altogether and was isolated.[4]

The Ghazal

The Ghazal is an ancient poetic form whose subject is love. Today it is known and practiced most prominently in the literature of South and Central Asia. However, in the late twentieth century, the ghazal began to be adopted as a poetic form by English-speaking poets.[5] The themes of the ghazal are fluid and often ambiguous. The poet expresses both the joy of love and the pain of hopeless separation. The love that the ghazal celebrates is an illicit, forbidden, and hopeless love. The object of love may be male or female, divine or human, sometimes human and divine at the same time. Mir Taqi Mir's poems usually speak of love as irresistible, all-consuming, and agonizing.

The classical ghazal must adhere to a strict form. The poem consists of five or more rhyming couplets with a revolving phrase that must be introduced in the first couplet toward the end of both lines of the couplet. The second line of the following couplets must conclude with the same phrase. Repetition creates the power of the ghazal. The rhyme scheme of the couplets is: aa, ba, ca, da, etc. The final words of the second line are usually repeated, rather than rhymed.

The form of the ghazal is rigidly fixed. But the poem should strive to surprise the audience with the various meanings that can be given to the same repeated phrase. The final couplet of the poem often, though not necessarily, includes the poet's name, allowing him to insert himself into the poem with a signature. The poet is traditionally male, expressing usually unrequited love for a young woman, a young man, or for God, or for all three.

The ghazal is not necessarily narrative in form or intent. The couplets of the poem may be discontinuous, or even unrelated. It is often the former. Each couplet can thus be regarded as a separate poem. The ghazal is held together by an overriding mood or emotion, whether sexual desire, fear of loss, despair, or spiritual longing for the beloved — either human or divine. However, there are ghazals that have a singular motif. These continuous form ghazals are referred to as *ghazal-e musalsal.*

The ghazal is traditionally performed before an audience as a song or a poem. It is not intended to simply stay on the page. Performance was often in the form of a competition, with different poets vying to win the approval of the crowd.

And so, the wit and the skill of the poet to rouse the emotions was paramount. The ghazal should surprise the audience with the skillful use of language, should stir sexual desire, but also startle the audience with its spiritual insight. The cheers of the audience mark a successful poem. Mir was a master of this theatrical performance. He sadly remembers his heyday in one of his ghazals:

> You see this grieving Mir, he was young once.
> His rhymes made men kick up a ruckus once.
>
> He hid his magic verses in these scrolls.
> They stared in awe when he read poems once.
>
> On any Delhi street his broken heart
> could stand and raise the Day of Judgment once.[6]

As noted, ghazals have been written in English by important poets. But translating the ghazal from its original language into English presents a particular challenge. Not all of Mir's poems are ghazals. But the goal of this volume was to craft translations of a small selection of Mir's ghazals into English that are successful as English poems on their own terms, while remaining as close and true to the form and meaning of the original Urdu ghazals as possible. Rhyme, repetition, and meter are such vital and integral aspects of Mir's ghazals — of all classical poetry — that the translators felt that both had to be acknowledged in English. Of course, repetition was vital, even if internal to the lines of the couplet. The scan of these Urdu ghazals could not be imitated. However, the translators substituted iambic pentameter, or sometimes iambic tetrameter, both familiar English conventions, for the traditional Urdu meter scheme. English has very few opportunities for rhyme as compared with Urdu. Yet, every effort was made to include rhyme prominently in the English versions. All of Mir's poems are untitled. The titles used in this volume have been added by the translators, another English convention.

Mir, The Sufi Poet

Mir Taqi Mir wrote his poems within a tradition of Sufi poetry that stretches back centuries before his time. He had absorbed the Sufi teachings of his father and would have been familiar with the great poets of this tradition, such as 'Attar (c.1146-1221), Sa'adi (1210-1291), Rumi (1207-1273) and Hafez (1325-1390). Sufism is a major movement within the Islamic tradition that, while not necessarily opposed to religious law and ritual practice, holds that the core and essence of religion is reunion with God, not observance of outward forms. The Sufis are mystics whose ultimate goal is spiritual enlightenment, which can be experienced in this world. It is the pursuit of such ecstatic experiences that preoccupies the Sufi. Ecstasy can be achieved through such practices as music, dance, repetition of the names of God, ascetic practices, and so forth. It is the goal of the Sufi poet to capture such experiences in words and communicate them in poems. But this is, of course, impossible since these mystic insights are transcendent, outside the realm of the material world. The Sufi poet must resort to traditional metaphors to suggest spiritual states. References to such tropes as madness, drunkenness, sexual longing, self-immolation, etc. are common in such poems.

A prominent, and sometimes controversial, element of Sufi poems is the need to violate the strictures of Muslim law, the *shari'a*, to achieve spiritual enlightenment. Wine is forbidden in Islam, for example, but it is universally used as a symbol of spiritual intoxication by the Sufis. Similarly, forbidden lust and illicit sex do the same.

In the poem "Wine Boy,"[7] included in this collection, Mir praises the *saqi*, the boy who serves the drink in the tavern, who brings the means of intoxication and is the object of sexual desire. But the wine boy is simultaneously a symbol of spiritual longing and enlightenment:

Wine boy! Without you we will never know
ourselves. Lost, we wander in our homeland.

Mir describes his mystic insight as a kind of overwhelming madness, a frantic love, that he can only hold down with chains.

The chains of reason hold me down, or I
would live insane — at frantic love's command.

But this experience is short lived and ephemeral. Soon it is only a memory, like a fold in his clothing that disappears when he changes position.

Mir, you were swept away by love. Now it's
just a ripple on your robe when you stand.

But Mir's poems about wine are not just allegorical and symbolic. He also describes the full-bodied experience of drunkenness that is in conflict with religion and decency. He confesses his sorry state openly. Still, his struggle with Islam continues.

It's not my fault if I can't walk a line.
So don't be angry now, for I am drunk.

The Friday prayer won't run away. Slow down,
damn it! Let me come too, though I am drunk.

Mir, what's this? Your soft words, your wild temper?
My lips can't argue with the glass. I'm drunk.[8]

Mir's poems about desire and romantic affairs follow a similar pattern. They are fully real and embody the human condition convincingly. Yet, Mir is aware of their violation of Islamic boundaries.. Surrounded by beautiful women who were not bound by Muslim strictures, Mir's lovers were often Hindus. He was aware of this transgression, which creates the tension in the poems:

The sad sighs of my heart. Eyes white, sweat red.
No cup. No wine. No air. No clouds for me.

No act. No show. No style. No miracle.
You are deadly in your simplicity.

Leave the idol house, Mir. You've known beauty.
Find the Ka'aba. But, there's no God in me.[9]

But Mir recognizes the inevitability, and perhaps even the necessity of transgression, hinting that it may be the will of God. For Sufis, it is the only means of salvation.

You walk out of the idol house now, Mir.
You'll run back when God brings her here once more. [10]

Mir, Poet Of Love

That Mir was quite the infidel, he was.
The first one to make love his creed, he was.[11]

The central theme and the animating force of all of Mir's poems is love, in all of its forms and conditions. This is not an idealized, metaphorical, or ethereal love. It is a fully carnal desire, a frankly sexual love, that Mir uses to explore the human condition.

Mir writes about every aspect of love, from the first stirrings of the heart to unbearable longing, frantic pursuit, joyful union, betrayal, separation, sadness, despair, and even love after death. But the poems are dark. Mir experiences love as pure misery. He loves because he cannot stop himself from loving. But his mood is one of tragedy and hopelessness. And yet, it is only love that he can write about. He finds it everywhere he looks. The subject of every poem is the lover—either himself as the miserable and forlorn suiter or the cruelty of the beloved whom he pursues. Though he can't explain it, love is his obsession.

How can I tell you what it is, this love?
It's a disease, it is a plague, this love.

Love — only love — exists. Look! Everywhere
the universe is bursting with this love.[12]

In many of his poems, Mir laments a lover he has lost and will never find again. She haunts him and sours all of the loves that have followed. She is the source of endless tears and sorrow. It is a wound that is never healed.

Now, highs and lows are all the same to me,
stomped in the earth like a footprint by fate.

My wary friends were wiser than I was.
Reckless me, locked behind this prison gate.

Don't ask about my loves. Talk about you!
I lost. My tales will just humiliate.[13]

This sadness seems to be a result of his tragic love affair with a married woman, the affair that caused his exile, his estrangement from his family, and his lifelong humiliation.

Nonetheless, Mir goes on loving, longing, and finding new lovers. Grief and sadness are constants, but so is love. Mir goes on loving through his tears. He can't explain why.

Love is just beginning, and I weep. Why? . . .

The land of heart will not turn green again.
Still, I sow seeds of my desire. Why?

These love stains on my skin will not come off.
Still, I wash the wounds that scar my chest. Why? [14]

The answer is complicated. As Mir pursues his loves, he cannot forget his first true lover. Nor can he fully ignore the dictates of Islamic law. He is filled with conflict and contradiction. Exposing this tension in verse, the poet writes masterful lines:

I chased her for long miles, but stopped to pray.
God! Even mad with love, I dared not sin.[15]

Mir's frantic lust collides with religious duty. Neither are abandoned.

So weak, I bore the grief of love and faith.
With ease, I lifted up both heavy weights.[16]

But for Sufis, the seeker cannot live in pursuit of love and at the same time live within the limits of law. Love destroys all boundaries and makes law and religion irrelevant. This is a theme common to all Sufi poets. Mawlana Rumi writes in one of his quatrains (rubaiyat):

On the seekers path, wise men/fools are one.
In this love, brothers and strangers are one.

Go on! Drink the wine of the Beloved!
In that faith, Muslims and pagans are one.[17]

The ultimate violation of the Muslim law is apostasy, the complete rejection of Islam as the pathway to salvation. Few Sufi mystics ever went this far. But Mir confesses that he has taken this last step. In despair, he writes as the final lines of a long poem:

Life is black and white now. From dawn to dark
I weep. Night to day, I am in tears now.

Why ask Mir his creed? Praying in the temple,
caste mark on his brow, he's left Islam now.[18]

This is only a temporary departure, or perhaps only an expression of extreme sorrow. But the poem stirs the reader to experience the poet's state of spiritual bankruptcy.

Bridging Time and Space

How is a translation of Mir's poems possible over a gulf of time and place and culture, substituting English words for Urdu words? But as we have said, poetry is not words. It is the language that we turn to when words fail. Poetry is, in fact, the attempt to move beyond words, to communicate states of mind and states of spirit that cannot be captured by language, but which nonetheless must be expressed. The poem only points or suggests. It does not delineate or explain. It must startle, demand attention, and conjure strong feelings in the reader. If it doesn't, then the poem is a failure. So, perhaps it is possible to find those emotions—across languages, across cultures, across time—and to translate poems that will move new readers. By some miracle of language, it is possible, but not by translating words. After all, technology has caught up with literal translation. Google Translator and other AI programs are now capable of producing perfectly acceptable translations into prose. But these machine translations fall flat. Their flaccid prose can invoke none of the emotion of the original. A good poem should cause goosebumps, tears, chills, a flash of sudden insight, or other responses. The translator of poetry must struggle to find the concepts, the music, and the images in a new language that can be crafted to the same effect as those in the original language.

This volume is the product of collaboration between a native Urdu speaker, Bilal A. Shaw, and an English-speaking poet, Anthony A. Lee, who knows no Urdu at all. Our method of translation began with Shaw making a literal translation into English of each line, preserving the original structure of the poem. The next step was for Lee to take those lines and rewrite them to ensure the construction of acceptable poems in English. The first drafts were then returned to the Urdu scholar for comment and correction; and then back and forth until both were satisfied with the results. The act of "translating" is a process accomplished through this interaction. The meaning of the Urdu must be understood by the poet who seeks to find words and images in English that will be as clear and as powerful as those in the original. The meaning of the poems and their cultural and historical contexts must be understood by the Urdu scholar, while the clarity and power of the English poem is ensured by the poet.

Of course, the quality of the result depends upon the knowledge of the Urdu speaker and the skill of the English poet. This method of translation is relatively uncommon in academia, which has traditionally relied on the unassisted scholar of languages to provide all translations of poetic texts. More recently, the necessity of collaboration has come to be appreciated. This method was pioneered successfully by Amin Banani, professor of Persian language, and the English poet Jascha Kessler, to translate the poems of Foruough Faroukzad, a modern Iranian poet.[19] Anthony A. Lee later collaborated with Banani and Kessler to bring into English the poems of Tahirih Qurratu'l-'Ayn, a nineteenth-century Iranian Babi poet and martyr beatified by Muhammad Iqbal.[20] Tony Barnstone and Bilal A. Shaw collaborated to produce a successful translation of selected ghazals of Ghalib, the premier nineteenth-century Urdu poet.[21]

All translations of Mir's poems should be startling and seductive, natural-sounding, and fascinating. They must call up a poetic world of their own, the mystic world of the Sufi poet, Mir Taqi Mir. These poems must be approached and read as poems, with full attention, but not as an academic project. Each poem invites us to enter a world that is unique and beyond time and space. We enter, as it were, another dimension where time stands still, we forget where we are sitting, and we find ourselves transfixed by the beauty of Mir's personal and mystical experiences, understood on no other terms but their own. We hope that these English translations will accomplish that goal for their audience as intensely, and indeed as ecstatically, as the original Urdu poems do for theirs.

References

[1] Cf. Gopi Chand Narang, *Hidden Garden*, trans. Surinder Deol (New York: Penguin, 2021) 32-3

[2] That is, Urdu poetry.

[3] *Mu'amlat-e-ishq* (The Stages of Love) and *Khwab o*

Khyal-e Mir (Mir's Vision), both written in the first person.

[4] This narrative of Mir's life draws heavily on the preface to Narang's the *Hidden Garden*.

[5] See, for example, famously, Agha Shahid Ali, *Ravishing Discontinuities: Real Ghazals in English* (Hanover: Wesleyan University Press, 2000).

[6] "He Was Young Once," p. 74.

[7] "Wine Boy!*," p. 67.

[8] "I'm Drunk," p. 75.

[9] "It's Over," p. 72.

[10] "Rejected," p. 80.

[11] "A New Creed," p. 102.

[12] "Love," p. 81.

[13] "Don't Ask," p. 83.

[14] "Love Is Just Beginning," p. 42.

[15] "Finished," p. 97.

[16] "Love and Faith," p. 86.

[17] "On the Seeker's Path," *Rumi: 53 Secrets from the Tavern of Love*, trans. Amin Banani, et al. (Ashland, OR: White Cloud Press, 2014) p. 3.

[18] "Finished," p. 97.

[19] *Bride of Acacias* (Delmar, NY: Caravan Books, 1982).

[20] *Tahirih A Portrait in Poetry: Selected Poems of Qurratu'l-'Ayn* (Los Angeles: Kalimat Press, 2005).

[21] *Faces Hidden in the Dust: The Selected Ghazals of Ghalib*, trans. Tony Barnstone and Bilal Shaw (Buffalo, NY, White Pine Press, 2021).

Translator's Note

The poems of Mir Taqi Mir are voluminous, making up six divans. We were able to find only one reference to a volume claiming to be his complete works, published by Oxford University Press. That book is now out of print. We were able to find a digitized copy of this divan at archive.org, however, searching this online repository does not always retrieve accurate results. It's also not clear whether in fact Oxford University Press had the complete divan to begin with.

Therefore, without an authoritative and critical collection of Mir's work, we had to rely on selective volumes of poems arranged by other scholars. For this volume, the translators relied on the Urdu texts found in K. C. Kanda's collection, *Mir Taqi Mir: Selected Poetry* (New Delhi: Sterling Publishers, 1998). This was a respected source. But as we were preparing this book for press, we had occasion to compare the Urdu texts found in Kanda's volume to versions of the same poems found online on the website Rekhta (rekhta.org). In some cases, we found discrepancies.

Some of the ghazals that Kanda published in Urdu aside his translations seem to be missing couplets that had somehow been removed. At least, there are alternate versions of these same ghazals online that appear to be more complete. It appears that Kanda shortened some of the ghazals, for reasons that are unclear. Perhaps at the insistence of his publisher. We have discovered the alternate versions for only some poems, because not all of Kanda's selections are found online. In cases where more complete ghazals have been found, we have restored the missing couplets in our translations. In these instances, we have departed from Kanda's Urdu texts in favor of the Rekhta version. We hope that this will provide the reader with a more accurate and complete translation of those poems into English and a better opportunity to appreciate Mir's genius.

The Translators

Contents

Three
Mir Goes on Loving

Four
Clasp Your Hand around Your Heart

Five
The Plague of Love

Six
There He Lies So Far Away

Seven
Finished

For my mother, *Yaqoot,*
the precious one.

For my Urdu teacher, *Nazir,*
the observant one.

For my wife, *Özden,*
the graceful one.

Bilal Shaw

For my wife, *Flor*

Anthony A. Lee

The Plague of Love

Selected Sufi Love Poems of Mir Taqi Mir

One

Now I'm in Love

Agony

I'm in love. So, where is patience?
Since my eyes met hers, where is sleep?

My restless dance shouts I'm a fool.
The lightning struck! Where is more jolt?

Until the letter comes, say what you will.
I have no answer yet. Where is my fate?

The veil between us is this life.
Without this life, where is that veil?

My eyes blood red with sleeplessness.
Poor drunken me! Where is my wine?

Love must slowly roast its lovers.
In hell, where is such agony?

My blackened heart and liver lie just here.
Where else could you burn black such nice kebabs?

Turned mad by your storybook face,
where will I find another book?

Mir, the house of love, it's open.
Where else can you, a beggar, live?

Love Is Just Beginning

Love is just beginning, and I weep. Why?
Just go on. See what happens, man! Why not?

Hear that? Sounds of the morning caravan.
So, move! They're leaving, fool. You're sleeping. Why?

The land of heart will not turn green again.
Still, I sow seeds of my desire. Why?

These love stains on my skin will not come off.
Still, I wash the wounds that scar my chest. Why?

Yet more precious than Joseph's hair is time!
And, Mir, you are wasting this rare thing. Why?

Do Something

It's a gamble, but you must do something.
You can't just sit here. You must do something.

Love speaks with only one tongue: Do something.
So, shout! Wail! Weep! But you must do something.

Why do you sit, hands in your lap, hopeless?
The caravan is leaving! Do something!

Should I kill someone or slit my own throat?
My tongue replies: Yes. You must do something.

Should I watch my chest bleed or write poems?
And he replies: Yes. You must do something.

If you can't pray to God, at least follow
your heart. But there's no time left. Do something!

You and I aren't friends. When this friend's heart comes
close to yours, of course it must do something.

Mir, it's not that you're old. You're just lazy.
You're young, by God's grace. So, go do something!

Share Your Sorrow

Don't wander alone with secret sorrow.
Share with me, your friend, your words of sorrow.

Madness overtakes me when I can't love.
But Mir! Why would she tell you her sorrows?

I Worship You

I worship you, and God knows that.
What you may think? Well, God knows that.

The agony of love is sweet.
Every wretched lover knows that.

Without her there's no life in me.
She's murdered me, but she knows that.

Beneath her hair, behind her veil,
what she wants, only she knows that.

You think I am a fraud like you?
My pleas aren't false. But you know that.

My prayers to God are treason now.
You slay your lovers. I know that.

Your earrings trap just innocents.
But Mughal children don't know that.

You're a spoiled and stupid child. But
you twist your lips well. You know that.

The way she walks kicks up a din.
Her lovers go mad. She knows that.

No fire, no ice can burn my heart
the way she burns me. I know that.

The torture I endure will end
when she sheds my blood. I know that.

Because you live inside my heart,
true love is there. But you know that.

Angels couldn't charm his shadow.
Then how could he know her like that?

When you're in love, Mir, you're ruined.
You gave away your heart, fool. You know that.

Pleasure

It is she alone who can bring me pleasure.
I want it now in my youth, this pleasure

This tasteless food—no joy drinking water .
Without her, there's no such thing as pleasure.

I'm Falling

Tonight, my tears fall down in streams, it seems.
The clouds of mercy weep regret, it seems.

You are naive if you think she's naive.
For me she is just false, or so it seems.

Standing, waiting, so weak outside her door,
I'm falling like a crumbling wall, it seems.

The beauty of the rose, the cypress too.
In her garden, they aren't my friends, it seems.

When can I show her that my love is true?
Her house is packed—like a bazaar, it seems.

Two

You Are Cruel

My Heart is Desolation

Who says you must do this, you must do that?
At least, leave a small space for the heart, please.

When that fair beauty walks in her tight robes,
holy men fold up their prayer rugs with ease.

What can I say? My heart is desolation.
This house collapsed in a pile of debris.

How long can I just gaze at love and colors?
Blood begins to fill my cheeks. Stop, please!

My colorless life holds some pleasures. But
when dawn's light breaks, midnight never leaves.

Long years I suffered. I saw such hard times.
She practiced all her cruelties as she pleased.

Some were flayed, some she tortured at the stake.
Now they regret they whispered their love pleas.

Let others pray while fevered storm clouds dance.
Saint! Now's your chance to sin as you may please!

Why did you show your face to me just then?
Mir glanced at you with lust, but now he leaves.

I Waited

You knew a hundred just like me,
but I could find no one like you.

A hundred things you said to me,
but I said none of them to you.

I tumbled half-way around the world,
but then I fell for only you.

You didn't see the world at all,
but knew I was not right for you.

Everyone came to claim your love,
but no one waited there for you.

As I waited for your love, I
tore out my heart from my chest, too.

They flashed like lightning, but fell mute.
I'm the only cloud that stayed true.

They all found rest in your garden.
For me, no rose or cypress dew.

Our friendship is proper and good.
But I love you, as I must do.

I know that you are always cruel.
Why did I give my heart to you?

Yes, every man who saw her face
collapsed, then made himself anew.

Mir, you alone could not get up,
broken, like a fallen statue.

Mad With Love

Why did I throw my whole life in harm's way?
What have I done? I gave my heart away.

I used to whisper words, or just sit still.
Those were good times! How things have changed today!

We swore to meet in dust and bathe in blood.
So, from her street how could I walk away?

You turned your gaze from me, and my life stopped.
Was that your lover's death, or just your play?

Mir talks to strangers now, stares at passersby.
"Yes, he stood here mad with love just yesterday."

My Funeral Pyre

This smoke, from where does it rise up?
From my heart and soul it rises up.

Is that the sky, or my scorched pyre?
At dawn, flames from my chest rise up.

Your place is in my heart. Don't leave.
No, from this home you can't rise up.

And where her flashing eyes will fall,
just in that place the storms rise up.

I have no hope you'll take me back,
if from your door I should rise up.

If I should leave your place, I swear,
it's from this world I will rise up.

Mir, love lies like a heavy stone.
You are too weak to lift it up.

When Will You See Me?

But when will you see Mir? Just me?
I know one day you'll see just me.

Please! Over here! Just glance this way.
Look at the things love lets us see.

The sweat that glistens on her face,
like dew drops on a rose. You see!

I saw the tears fill in my eyes.
It was her smile I longed to see.

I'm going away, if truth be told.
I'll soon be close to death. Praise be!

My courage? A mere drop of blood,
though my heart pumps with love in me.

There are still delights in you, Mir.
Just think about it. You will see.

Three

Mir Goes on Loving

Inside

A thousand hopes I hide inside.
I crush my heart, hide it inside.

Like flashing lightning, eager there,
I hide a heart that leaps inside.

You give your favors to my foe,
while I keep your love deep inside.

That glance, those words, broke your promise.
Fine! I still hold your name inside.

Where is a song sweeter than mine?
The rest are lip and style inside.

Some other girl may steal my heart.
Now that's my only hope inside.

Even so Mir goes on loving.
He has the right. He's young inside.

Her Magic Spell

Now my life is like an empty bubble,
is like a mirage, a desert bubble.

What can I say? The thin edge of her lip
is like the softness of a rose petal.

Time and again, my journey to her door
is like the ache of anguish and trouble.

Finally I speak. I can hear my voice.
But it's like a house collapsed in rubble.

Mir, your drunken eyes, half-closed, dream of sins.
It's like when wine casts up its magic spell.

Burn

If I cry, Earth and Air will burn.
The blue slope of the sky will burn.

Don't ask Mir of love's cruelty.
If he cries, the cosmos will burn.

On Your Street

I longed for your love, but you were cruel.
Your heart's not made of wax. It's only stone.

This love-burn scars my heart. Who is the one
for whom I saw you leave in haste from home?

No trembling lover will return. He'll come
back dead, if to your street he dares to roam.

My heart lies crushed and empty now, as if
crowds rushed out from it and left me alone.

My falling tears, the gushing of my blood,
my sliced liver, and half my broken heart.

Each I did endure so long, and better
than what that enemy, my eye, has shown.

Mir, you meant to write just a word or two.
Your short, sweet lines turned into a sad tome.

Your Treason

I was fire when love ignited me.
Now, I am nothing but burnt ash and dust.

Our lives are like a fading drop of dew.
One breath, and we are gone in the next gust.

I can't thank you enough for your treason.
My only grief is you betrayed my trust.

Enough with all your pride, your snobbery!
What have I done that earned me your disgust?

Look! They're lifting your lovers' coffins.
Come sit and watch this fine parade. You must!

So now it seems Mir is the only one.
The sole survivor of forgotten lust.

Mir's Poems

Mir is a river. Just hear him recite!
O God! O God! What thought! What art! What flow!

I spin my verse like magic. Yet, all my
mystic poems are lost in dust below.

I begged and begged. You never listened once.
My humble soul ignored by your ego.

I wrote a verse for you on every leaf.
And Spring itself was envious, I know.

Look there! Each fallen forest blade conceals
the message of my love in autumn's glow.

At night, I would cry out my sad story.
But you slept through it all. You missed my show.

The requiems I wrote inside my heart!
They saw my grief in Delhi streets also.

In youth, I was all kindness and good works.
A tender boil, I burst with every blow.

And now I'm gone. So, send up your lament.
Too bad. While I was here you didn't know.

Four

Clasp Your Hand around Your Heart

Wine Boy!*

Now your tongue is curled up like a rosebud.
You've left the garden with your shriveled hands.

Clasp your palm around your heart when you cry.
In such a storm, your lamp will die unmanned.

Leave my mouth closed when I'm in my grave
or, in my shroud, you'll waken love's demands.

Don't scorch yourself listening to my woes.
Head to toe, I'm on fire where I stand.

Wine boy! Without you we will never know
ourselves. Lost, we wander in our homeland.

The chains of reason hold me down, or I
would live insane—at frantic love's command.

Where did the candles go? Did the moths die?
Once this garden was blazing with life, man.

Even though I'm a poet, not a hack,
I fear the rhymes my friends recite offhand.

Mir, you were swept away by love. Now it's
just a ripple on your robe when you stand.

*Literally, *saqi*. The *saqi* is the young cupbearer who serves wine to the customers in a tavern. In Sufi imagery, he brings intoxication and is the object of longing and erotic desire. As such, he can represent the spirit, or even stand in as a symbol for God himself.

My Grief

This grief has pushed the last breath from my lips.
Look here! In shock, how now my heartbeat skips.

I meant to write a verse, I'll write a book.
I can't help writing more when passion slips.

See! My demolished heart is such a sight.
Grief has crushed a mansion's workmanship.

Those ruby lips of yours are on display.
But they're not true. They're just your showmanship.

You are so near to me, and yet so far.
Who do you give your trust, your true friendship?

I will love, and I will die from this disease,
this distance from the one whom I worship.

Here I sit fallen down into the dust.
There she sits proud, decked out each fingertip.

Since *Majnun*'s* death . . . since then, I've lost my mind.
Since that madman died, I can't find my grip.

**Majnun* is the heroic lover in Persian literature who spent his life in madness, pining away for his beloved *Layli.*

Too Dear

But who is not in love with you? I know
too much about this, so I've fallen ill.

You are so dear. Whoever sees you will
sell his life and end up a buyer still.

Wipe Your Tears

You weep with such a racket, Mir!
How are your neighbors going to sleep?

I'll leave this world in tears, wailing.
When I'm gone, for me clouds will weep.

For how long can you wipe my face,
my friend? All I can do is weep.

My heart cries out in agony,
so loud, caravan bells sound weak.

Go on! Curse my new enemy.
But not a word to me. Don't speak.

Mir! Wipe the tears from your lashes,
and let that string of old pearls break.

My Heart Ablaze

Just see what happened here before our days.
Ignorant, man will never mend his ways.

What can I say of what I see in you?
Your style! Look how she walks and how she plays.

My heart is gone, my patience, my life too.
Grief has taken everything. Nothing stays.

You were cruel to ask what I want from you.
Just the joy in your eyes, your loving ways.

"Wretch and rake! Wanderer!" Those are my names.
That's what the people call me, anyways.

I can't report all the talk about you.
You won't hear what I say. You're in a daze.

I saw your face—my loss, my desire.
It killed me. But it set my heart ablaze.

But, Mir, you left this world without a thing.
Look at the treasures the world still displays.

It's Over

We rarely meet now. What is there to see?
You walk princess proud. Nothing's left of me.

Morning breezes, the fragrance of red rose
vanish at a glance. No fidelity.

I find no fault with you. God protect me!
I grieve for my fate. Why are you angry?

Nightingale, don't sing while I am weeping.
I tell you this each night. Don't dare mock me.

The sad sighs of my heart. Eyes white, sweat red.
No cup. No wine. No air. No clouds for me.

No act. No show. No style. No miracle.
You are deadly in your simplicity.

Leave the idol house, Mir. You've known beauty.
Find the *Ka'aba.** But, there's no God in me.

*The shrine in Mecca toward which all Muslims turn to say their daily prayers.

Hell-Fire

Look! Both your ruby lips are crimson red,
and both of them breathe out hell-fire and dread.

How can you hide your charms behind a veil?
Or hide your eyes, the two suns in your head?

My heart, my eyes, found two homes inside your
temple. Soon both were desolate and dead.

Don't ask me more. See how the flames of grief
consume my heart, my liver. I am dead.

Her eyes flash a hundred different targets.
Darting to places where the wine has led.

My eyes and heart now boil in agony.
Fire and water in one riverbed.

Back then, my eyes were like two waterfalls.
It seems they were just a mirage, instead.

He Was Young Once

You see this grieving Mir, he was young once.
His rhymes made men kick up a ruckus once.

He hid his magic verses in these scrolls.
They stared in awe when he read poems once.

On any Delhi street his broken heart
could stand and raise the Day of Judgment once.

Yes, he was sad, but no wet sod. He was
wind, tornado, the scourge of the earth once.

How many times I tried to catch a glimpse
of flowers blooming on my grave, just once.

How I neglected my defeated heart!
It just lay lost in some dark corner once.

I'm Drunk

My friends, forgive me, please, for I am drunk.
Pour me an empty cup, for I am drunk.

And on the next round, give me just a sip.
Don't fill my blurry eyes, for I am drunk.

No need to listen to my garbled verse.
Just tell me what you please, for I am drunk.

Now, hold my hand the way you hold your glass
and walk with me a while, for I am drunk.

It's not my fault if I can't walk a line.
So don't be angry now, for I am drunk.

The Friday prayer won't run away. Slow down,
damn it! Let me come too, though I am drunk.

Mir, what's this? Your soft words, your wild temper?
My lips can't argue with the glass. I'm drunk.

Five

The Plague of Love

Lord! Protect Them

O Lord! Protect them from the pain of love.
Kill them! But save them from this plague of love.

Jail them! Chain them! Let them die in prison!
But don't let them commit the sin of love.

Rejected

The world brings troubles more than I can bear.
I can't lift my feeble self off the floor.

My heart brings me to her street yet again.
I bring myself to very dust once more.

My lovers died before the start of time.
What passions can they bring now to my door?

She scorns the trace of love saved in my heart,
though I show her the world's black empty core.

My heart can't hold one extra drop of blood,
yet it brings me the universe, and more.

You walk out of the idol house now, Mir.
You'll run back when God brings her here once more.

Love

How can I tell you what it is, this love?
It's a disease, it is a plague, this love.

Love—only love—exists. Look! Everywhere
the universe is bursting with this love.

Love is my lover. Love is my beloved.
And love itself delights inside this love.

This love makes its own law. Sometimes love is
the believer. Sometimes God is this love.

Who has ever reached his aim without love?
My wish is this love. My goal is this love.

But no one really wants this sort of love.
See! It's just like a bastard child, this love.

Mir, your life is looking so weak and pale.
Can you say you have ever been in love?

Shame and Joy

My friend, no one has known the shame I've known,
and this my worst enemy will concede.

Come! Let's visit the graves of these paupers.
See what they've suffered here with no misdeed.

In the valley of love, you'll lose your heart.
It won't birth back again, nor beat, nor bleed.

Friend don't build your home in this wasteland.
Every city will turn to dust and seed.

Every drop that falls flows toward a river.
Every part returns to the whole indeed.

A hundred arrows from her eyelashes
pierced my chest—but still I didn't bleed.

Mir, you will never know such joy again.
Now that mad love forever will recede.

Don't Ask

By then the caravan was miles away.
Yes, I know I woke up a bit too late.

Now highs and lows are all the same to me,
stomped in the earth like a footprint by fate.

My wary friends were wiser than I was.
Reckless me, locked behind this prison gate.

Don't ask about my loves. Talk about you!
I lost. My tales will just humiliate.

Look! He was carefree as a daffodil.
Those years of grief have brought him to this state.

Wasteland

As if in a painting, the people stare.
Eyes wide open, but they are unaware.

Mir, who can ever live in this wasteland?
Walls, doors fallen. The houses in despair.

A Smile

I whispered to the rose: Time to open!
Embrace the nightingale! Dawn has broken.

But there is only time for a brief smile.
Then, she too hides her face in her bosom.

Love and Faith

So weak, I bore the grief of love and faith.
With ease, I lifted up both heavy weights.

If my tears of blood fall on this wasteland,
this desert dust would bloom again with haste.

I told my cruel friend: "Now, my love has gone."
She said, with spite: "I don't control your fate."

I stored up all my stock in faith and love.
But no one bought my wares. That's my sad state.

How did Urdu verse attain such heights?
Mir exalted every line he could create.

Real Life

I told myself I'd have a lot to say
to that crazy Mir if we met somewhere.

Yesterday, I found him in the desert.
He, in so much pain, on his way somewhere.

I followed after him and said, "Poor soul!
Why don't you have a place to stay somewhere?

Why run away from ease and comfort here?
You know you must find a real life somewhere?"

I vexed him good, so then he said, "Do you
have a real home in the city somewhere?"

Now, I've forgotten where, but I know this.
A wise man wrote this saying down somewhere:

"Even if you love your house, free your soul.
Should a pilgrim want to settle down somewhere?"

Many live and die with lofty thoughts, Mir.
They disappeared without a trace somewhere.

Six

There He Lies So Far Away

He Was in Love

He was in love with you, like me.
So young and beautiful, so true.

Once, he broke down, wept, and said, "Mir!
Please, no more tales of woe from you."

Until He Comes

Long have my tears been falling. Still they come!
If my tears stop falling, my blood will come.

I can still control myself, until he comes.
Then, I lose my mind, and no sense will come.

Patience used to be my only friend here.
But now, he too is one who will not come.

My heart has lost all trace of its desire.
Just gone. No wonder now my tears have come.

It's all still here in this full heart, my friend.
But no verses on my lips. They won't come.

There he lies so far away . . . Poor sad Mir,
without his love, this poem will not come.

The Secret

I couldn't keep this secret of mine.
None understood this plea of mine.

Like tinkling bells of caravans,
far from you, loneliness is mine.

Travelers! I am here alone,
you don't know this sorrow of mine.

I am so far from whom I loved.
I wasted this good life of mine.

Without you, thoughts are vagabonds.
How they wander! These thoughts of mine.

Can't you see anything, Mir? Just
his face, where I cast this gaze of mine.

I'm Gone

I came begging, but with these words I'm gone.
Smile, man! I said a prayer for you! I'm gone.

I swore, "Without you there's no hope for life!"
No point. And faithful to that pledge, I'm gone.

Once I gazed at your face so hopelessly.
But now, I cannot find a trace. You're gone.

How many days I longed to roam your lane!
At last I left, and bathed in blood, I'm gone.

The day I saw you, it just drove me mad.
I can't stand this separation. I'm gone.

My forehead on the ground, again, again.
I bowed myself before you, now I'm gone.

I loved you. I worshipped you, my idol.
I saw you as a god of men. I'm gone.

I spent my life fretting over ghazals.
Well, I raised up this art, and now I'm gone.

Six

Finished

Finished

Long last, my restless heart brings me down now.
I failed. My schemes have come to nothing now.

In youth, I wept. Now old, my eyes run dry.
Awake all night, it's dawn. I'm sleeping now.

You do just as you please. So, why blame me?
Why should I have to know right from wrong now?

The world knells at your door now. Bandits, thieves,
liars, sly or rude, send you their prayers now.

So, where is Mecca? Which way should I pray?
Her lovers chant their prayers on her street now.

And tell me what's forbidden, what's allowed.
Which holy garment do I put on now?

Last night in the tavern, the holy man,
sold his shirt, his pants, his cloak now.

And then I saw him pawn his prayer cap, too.
Naked, he sits praying in the mosque now.

I chased her for long miles, but stopped to pray.
God! Even mad with love, I dared not sin now.

To catch that frantic deer was such a task!
The skill to calm her rage, a miracle now.

I clenched her silver arms, then let them go.
Why did I trust her words? I'm alone now.

Life is black and white now. From dawn to dark
I weep. Night to day, I am in tears now.

Why ask Mir his creed? Praying in the temple,
caste mark on his brow, he's left Islam now.

Just a Dream

Mir! It is just a dream, this world today.
Soon, all those seated here will fly away.

You opened your eyes. Now, open your ears!
One wing flap, and the world will pass away.

I Used to Sin

I strolled in gardens, once upon a time.
Roamed like a river, once upon a time.

My heart's high fever found so many friends.
They nursed my illness, once upon a time.

As long as she controlled her restless ways,
I restrained myself, once upon a time.

When I was young, I used to sin. Stayed late
in temples and mosques, once upon a time.

The flames of love leapt up, consumed my soul.
This liver boiled inside, once upon a time.

And now, my faithless heart has brought me down.
I could bear love's pain, once upon a time.

Mir, you're done. Where you sat, they'll say: "He burned
and told stories there, once upon a time."

My Heart Dims

This mirror stares at each and every face.
So, suddenly, why is it so amazed?

At early nightfall, my heart dims and dies,
just like a poor man's lamp that's filled halfways.

The tavern boys were in a nasty mood,
but this old man made his escape unscathed.

Now, flowers push up through my hollow eyes,
my hands hold daffodils in bright bouquets.

I am an empty bubble, stingy, weak.
And there you stand, your beggar bowl upraised.

You clouds! Take these tears streaming from my eyes
and flood a vast expanse with your tideways.

But who can stand to listen to Mir's tales?
The party's mood has changed from that these days.

Farhad's Lament*

With his shovel on my grave, *Farhad* said,
"Oh, my beloved teacher, you are dead."

"Alive, how could I be free of sorrow?
My wretched heart is tangled here," I said.

Don't fret about building up your mansions.
You cannot know when this life will unthread.

Look here at the wasteland where I live now.
I don't have dust to pour upon my head.

Don't you hear it? Hold on a while. Listen!
After me, such wailing will not be heard.

Everywhere it seems the birds are singing.
The hunter's woodland garden's my homestead.

I die again each day, and ask myself
when will I flee this prison-life I dread?

*The tale of *Farhad* and *Shirin* is one of the classical love stories of Persian literature. In the first lines of this poem, Mir suggests that he was the one who taught *Farhad* how to love.

A New Creed

That Mir was quite the infidel, he was.
The first one to make love his creed, he was.

You're Not a Poet

The God of favors favored me. From dust,
from nothing, he gave me a human look.

Don't say you're a poet, Mir. You just took
all your sadness and put it in a book.

Whisper!

I knew sorrows. But then I lost my heart.
So strange, so tragic to watch it depart.

Shhh! Whisper when you're near Mir's resting place.
Weeping, sobbing, he found the sleep he sought.

Bibliography

Ghalib. *Faces Hidden in the Dust: Selected Ghazals of Ghalib.* Trans. Tony Barnstone and Bilal Shaw. Buffalo, NY: White Pines Press, 2021.

Forough Farrukhzad. *Bride of Acacias Delmar.* NY: Caravan Books, 1982.

Mir Taqi Mir. *Mir Taqi Mir: Selected Poetry.* Trans. K. C. Kanda. New Delhi: Sterling Publishers, 1998.

Mir Taqi Mir. *Divan-e-Mir Farsi.* Oxford University Press. Archive.org,

https://archive.org/details/divanimirfarsi/mode/2up.

__________. *The Hidden Garden.* Ed. Gopi Chand Narang. Trans. Surinder Deol. New York: Penguin, 2021.

__________. *Selected Ghazals and Other Poems.* Trans. Shamsur Rahmsn Faruqi. Cambridge: Harvard University Press, 2019.

Rekhta.org, www.rekhta.org.

Rumi. *Rumi: 53 Secrets from the Tavern of Love.* Ed. And trans. Amin Banani. Los Angeles: Kalimat Press, 2014.

Nirala Series

A Series of Contemporary Writing

Dancing in Place: *New Poems*
S. Renay Sanders
ISBN ISBN 81-8250-048-6 2019 pp. 64 Paper Demy

Blue Fan Whirring : *Poems*
Mike Jurkovic
ISBN 978-8182500969 2019 pp. 160 Paper

The Second Buddha Walk:
Inspired by The Second Buddha ,
Master of Time Exhibit at Rubin Museum, New York
Yuyutsu Sharma
ISBN 978-8182500983 2019 pp. 52 Paper Demy

Imagined Secrets: *New Poems*
Robert Scotto
ISBN 978-81825000442019 pp. 79 Paper Demy

The Tin Man
David B. Austell
ISBN 9-788182-500792 2019 pp. 320 Hard Demy

All Vows:
New & Selected Poems
David B. Axelrod
ISBN 978-8182500822 2016 pp. 194

The Dhimals: Miraculous Migrants of Himal:
An Anthropological Study of a Nepalese Ethnic Group
Murari P. Regmi
ISBN 9788182500082 2016 pp. 294 Rs. 295

A Blizzard In My Bones: New York Poems
Yuyutsu RD Sharma
ISBN 81-8250-070-2 2016 pp.134 Pape

Letters from a Sacred Mountain Place:
A Journey through the Nepal Himalayas – Photographs and Text by **Diane Frank**
ISBN 81-8250-095-8 2018 Hard Cover pp. 144

Path to Excellence:
A Memoir by India's Distinguished Academician Pritam B. Sharma
ISBN : 81-8250-0907 2017 Hard Cover pp. 358

Word Has It : *Poems*
Ruth Danon
ISBN 81-8250-097-4 2018 Paperback pp. 85

Eternal Snow: *A Worldwide Anthology of One Hundred Twenty Five Poetic Intersections with Himalayan Poet Yuyutsu RD Sharma*
Edited by **David Austell & Kathleen D Gallagher**
ISBN : 81-8250-088-5 2017 Paperback pp. 309

Cats, Love & Other Surprises
by **Otis Kidwell Burger**
Illustrations by **Katherine Burger**
ISBN : 978-8182500891 2017 Hardback pp. 65 RS. 1495

Making of The Indian Muse
Context and Perspectives in Indian Poetry in English
Edited by **Goutam Karmakar**
ISBN 978-8182500273 2019 pp. 430

Ritual: The Magical Perspective
Efficacy an the Search for Inner Meaning
Luc Sala
ISBN 9-788182-500617 2014 Hard pp. 832 Rs.1495

Your Kiss is a River
Poems of Love, Food and Life
Carolyn Wells
ISBN 9-788182-500532 2016 pp.56 Hard Rs 195

Inside the Shell of the Tortoise
Poems written in India and Nepal
A Spanish English Edition
Veronica Aranda
Translated by Claudia Routon with Yuyutsu Sharma
ISBN 9-788182-500686 2016 pp. 56 Hard Rs.395

Space Cake, Amsterdam
& Other Poems from Europe and America
Yuyutsu RD Sharma
ISBN-81-8250-059-1 2014 Hard pp. 110

Milarepa's Bones, Helambu
33 New Poems
Yuyutsu RD Sharma
ISBN-81-8250-032-X 2012 Hard pp. 64

Little Creek
& Other Poems
David Austell
ISBN 81-8250- 031-1 2011 Hard pp. 200 Rs.495

The Mystery Over Lord Buddha's Roots
An Analysis of the Mystery of the Shakya Kingdom
Mitsuaki KOJIMA
ISBN 9-788182-500563 2014 Hard pp. 165 Rs.495

Dada Poetry
An Introduction
William Seaton
Foreword by **Timothy Shipe**
ISBN-9-788182-500358 2013 Hard pp.112 Rs. 395

Libraries, Information Centers &
Information Professionalism in Nepal
Madhusudan Karki
ISBN 9-788182-500372 2012 Hard pp. 348 Rs. 895

Student Politics & Democracy in Nepal
Meena Ojha
ISBN 9-788182-500259 2010 Hard pp. 411 Rs. 795

The Yeti
Spirit of Himalayan Forest Shamans
Larry G. Peters
ISBN 9-788182-500525 2014 Hard pp.128 Rs. 350

Folk Tales of Sherpa and Yeti
Collected by Shiva Dhakal
Adapted by Yuyutsu RD Sharma
ISBN 9-788182-500624 2014 Paper pp.125 Rs. 350

Annapurnas & Stains of Blood
Life, Travel &Writing on a page of Snow
Yuyutsu R D Sharma
ISBN 9-788182-500129 2010 Hard pp. 200 Rs. 495

Trance, Initiation & Psychotherapy in Nepalese Shamanism
Essays on Tamang and Tibetan Shamanism
Larry G.Peters
ISBN 9-788182-500532 2014 Paper pp. 412 Rs. 995

Tamang Shamans
An Ethnopsychiatric Study of Ecstasy and Healing in Nepal
Larry G. Peters
ISBN 9-788182-500099 2007 Paper pp. 179 Rs. 295

The Pokhara Valley
A Traveler's Guide
ISBN 9-788182-500198 2010 Paper pp. 202 Rs. 595